Think about it...
Senses

Harry Cory Wright

W
FRANKLIN WATTS
LONDON • SYDNEY

What do you think this person has been eating?
What do you think it might have tasted like?

How might this water feel?

What would it be like to touch these stones?

How does this fire make you feel?

What sounds
might you hear
standing under
this tree?

Try to describe this jelly.

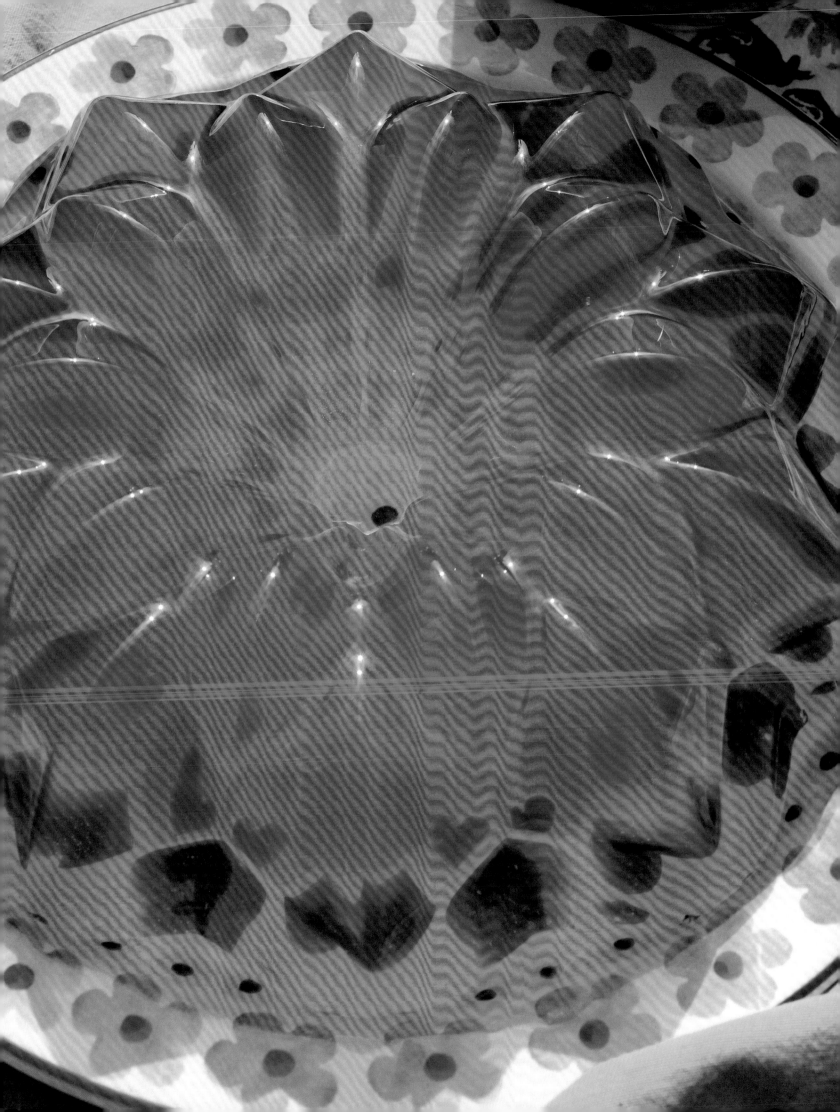

What sounds might you hear...

if you stood in this street for a while?

If you stayed here for ten minutes...

what is the first thing you might hear?

What might it feel like to hold
this jar of fish?

How do you think
it might smell under
this bridge?

What sounds might
you hear?

What might this rose smell like?

Think of a 'made up' word for the sound that this horn might make.

What do you think it would have been like here as this firework went off?

What would
these feel like?
Would you like
to hold them?

What might these
taste like?

Senses

What do things taste like? What do they look like? Why do we like some foods and not others? How do the things we look at and hear make us feel and how important are they? Our senses are vital to how we perceive and engage with the world around us and here we explore the essence of how we begin to use these 'antennae'. Quite quickly it will become apparent that no two people will see, hear or feel the same things.

A framework for exploration

'What's going on in this picture?' is a question that is asked by children and adults alike whenever presented with a photograph. Usually the answer is in the caption. But what if we ask questions rather than provide answers? What if there is no right answer? The photographs in this book are intended to be starting points for children to explore ideas. Remember, there are no rules here, let alone any right answers – children can take a simple idea and run with it as far as they wish.

The teacher or parent should use his or her judgment to decide the appropriate depth of discussion according to the abilities of the child. Some children may describe only what they see in the picture in clear sentences. Other children should be able to extend the themes and offer in depth explanations and opinions. Ideas for expanding each theme are listed below in 'Talk about', but you may also ask some general questions on the theme of senses such as: How many different senses are being used here?

What do you think this person has been eating? What do you think it might have tasted like? (pages 2–3)
This is my daughter's tongue after eating one of those amazing sour sweets with added colour. Not that good for you perhaps, but great fun. Find out how many of the children have tried sweets like these. Do they like or dislike them? Why?
Talk about: • why it looks fun and unusual • what is in it • what is it that makes us able to taste things • why we go 'yuck' to food that is blue • why too many sweets are bad for us.

How might this water feel? (page 4)

This pond belongs to a friend of mine and in the summer it is wonderful to swim here. The land is very chalky and that's what gives it a creamy look. It was a warm day in August and I remember the light in the trees above. There were fish in the pond and dragonflies.
Talk about: • how different types of water (salt, fresh) feel on the skin • what swimming feels like • how it feels if salt water gets into the eyes • keeping safe around water.

What would it be like to touch these stones? (page 5)

This is at Stonehenge. I have rarely photographed stones that have such a presence and feeling of bigness.
Talk about: • what the stones may make you feel • what it is like to be next to something so big • the feel of the surface of the stones.

How does this fire make you feel? (pages 6–7)

This fire was in a little hut on an otherwise deserted island in the Western Isles of Scotland. It was very warming on a cold day.
Talk about: • why fires make us feel warm • what is it about being warm that makes us feel better • why fire can be dangerous • keeping safe near fires, both indoors and outside.

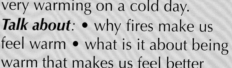

What sounds might you hear standing under this tree? (pages 8–9)

Looking up into this tree was like looking into another world. There were birds flying around, insects

flitting about and it was all full of light and air.
Talk about: • what would happen as the breeze blew through it • good describing words for the sound of the breeze in the tree, such as rustling, crackling, swishing, whispering • what animals might spend time in the tree • what the smell of the place might be like • how bird song makes them feel • why birds sing.

Try to describe this jelly. (pages 10–11)

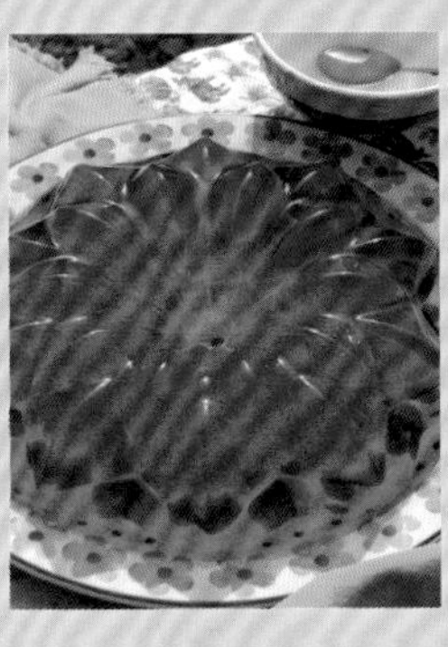

We made this jelly on a warm day in the spring. It was a big mould that used six packets of jelly. Describing a jelly can use all the senses.
Talk about: • what it might smell, taste and feel like in the mouth • what it would have looked like as it was carried outside to be photographed • what it would look like after we had begun to eat it • what it feels like to push a spoon into jelly.

What sounds might you hear... if you stood in this street for a while? (pages 12–13)

Think of all the things going on here! Where is everyone going? What are they in the middle of doing? Who might be working in the building at the back of the picture? We can see cranes, cameras, bicycles, traffic lights, different shoes on the pavement and roadworks.
Talk about: • how sounds are different in urban and country places • what you might see inside some of the windows • where might the loudest sound be coming from • the sounds they like/ dislike • exciting sounds in the city, such as parades; scary sounds – sirens (police, fire brigade, etc).

If you stayed here for ten minutes... what is the first thing you might hear? (pages 14–15)

This was a very calm and peaceful morning. The lido is in fact quite close to the sea and you could hear all manner of coastal sounds; seagulls, boat engines and some road traffic. It could be anywhere, of course, and what makes this picture interesting is what might be happening the other side of the wall.
Talk about: • what might it be like here later in the day • how the mood might change • places they find really peaceful • what it feels like to be silent for ten minutes.

What might it feel like to hold this jar of fish? (pages 16–17)

These fish were found on a beach in Scotland. We were very excited by the way the fish flitted about in the jar. It was sunny, bright and warm. The sand was very coarse and granular – all fresh, clean and salty.
Talk about: • how sand feels on the beach • how it feels to walk across sand on a hot day • what other things have a coarse texture • the smells and sounds of the beach • ways of describing the bodies of the fish including their colour, texture etc.

How do you think it might smell under this bridge? What sounds might you hear? (pages 18–19)

This part of the River Tweed is tidal and soon the water level will be much higher. This of course happens twice a day. My daughter is looking at the camera. She remembers the sounds as being quite echoing. There were cars moving over the bridge and some pigeons cooing amongst the concrete and steel.
Talk about: • reflections in the water and how they differ from the object • what the children might be doing • what the bridge might be used for • the feel of the muddy bank underfoot • playing near rivers and the potential dangers.

What might this rose smell like? (pages 20–21)

The smell from a rose like this is perhaps the most simple and pleasing smell I can think of. This rose is from the garden of a house we used to live in and every spring this rose was the most exciting to see in bloom.
Talk about: • why flowers usually smell nice • favourite smells • the texture of the rose petals and leaves and if they've ever felt them • the combination of colours in the rose petals.

Think of a 'made up' word for the sound that this horn might make. (pages 22–23)

I bought this horn from a junk shop because it looked so funny. It makes a sharp and annoying noise that gives me a fright every time the children squeeze it. It seems to say a mixture of things like 'wake up', 'pay attention' or 'stop it'. It's a very bossy noise.

Talk about: • funny sounds and words to describe them • things that make loud sounds • sounds that can scare us • things that make quiet sounds.

What do you think it would have been like here as this firework went off? (pages 24–25)

We set this firework off in the Outer Hebrides on a very quiet evening. It made a lot of noise but only for a short moment. The people on the left set it off for me. It disturbed the birds and they made a lot of noise of their own afterwards, but it soon settled down again.

Talk about: • why people enjoy fireworks • think of words to describe the noise and their effect in the sky • when we use fireworks • what other noises disturb things • dangers of fireworks.

What would these feel like? Would you like to hold them? (pages 26–27)

This is my son holding some snails on a wet day in the countryside. They moved very slowly around his hand like they were exploring and although he said it felt quite strange it wasn't a horrible feeling.

Talk about: • things you wouldn't like to touch and why not • things that feel strange to touch • why snails have slime • why snails have shells.

What might these taste like? (pages 28–29)

This shop in France had the most delicious pastries. They looked like they were made with great care by someone who knew how to make food look very tasty.

Talk about: • which of the pastries you would most and least like to eat • how you get food to look and taste good • favourite foods and why they are so special • why some foods are 'treats' that we shouldn't eat all the time • where the cakes may come from and why different countries have different foods.

First published in 2009
by Franklin Watts

Copyright © Harry Cory Wright 2009

Franklin Watts
338 Euston Road
London NW1 3BH

Franklin Watts Australia
Level 17/207 Kent Street
Sydney, NSW 2000

Series editor: Sarah Peutrill
Art director: Jonathan Hair
Consultant: Sue Graves

Dewey number: 612.8

ISBN 978 0 7496 8850 9

Printed in China

Franklin Watts is a division of Hachette Children's Books, an Hachette UK company.

www.hachette.co.uk